The Dog's Di....

The Dog's Dinner is an excellent little book that is perfectly suited to little people in need of a great big Savior.

TIM CHALLIES

Blogger at www.challies.com

Sometimes Jesus says things that are hard to understand—hard for children and adults. This book puts one of those hard things Jesus said in context of the whole Bible so both children and adults can understand!

NANCY GUTHRIE

Author of Seeing Jesus in the Old Testament Bible Study Series

An artful, luminous retelling of Jesus' graced encounter with the Canaanite woman — that is sure to delight little hearts and fill them with the Bread of Life.

KENT AND BARBARA HUGHES

Authors and conference speakers from Wheaton College Church, Illinois

Looking back from Genesis and forward to heaven, O'Donnell teaches important lessons about God's goodness, power and salvation that will open the eyes and ears of children. Get one for children around you!

JON M. DENNIS

Co-founding pastor of Holy Trinity Church Downtown Chicago

The Dog's Dinner

A Story of Great Mercy and Great Faith from
Matthew 14-15

Douglas Sean O'Donnell
Illustrated by Gail Schoonmaker

This is a book about food. And a dog, of course.

God has always loved his people. (Just like He loves you!) And He has shown His love in many, many different ways. One way is through

Food!

Think about the Garden of Eden. That was the home of Adam and Eve. Do you remember what God gave them?

He gave them a whole garden, filled with beautiful and delicious food.

Imagine all the apples and oranges and
grapes they got to eat!

Then think about the Promised Land. That was the home God gave the Israelites. It was filled with all kinds of yummy foods. Imagine eating the sweetest honey and drinking the purest milk.

Finally, think of the wilderness. That was the place where God's people lived because they disobeyed God's Word. But even in the wilderness God fed his starving people! He gave them bread from heaven. It was fresh. It was sweet. Imagine that warm and wonderful bread melting in your mouth.

Before Jesus was born, God's people believed a Savior was coming. He was coming to save them from every bad thing in the world—like sin and sickness, and death and the devil.

And they knew when this Savior came, something great would happen. . . . They would eat! Now, that might sound funny to you. But it's true. Yes, when God promised a Savior, He also promised a special meal. So, it's no surprise that when Jesus came to the Promised Land He showed God's love to God's people—with food!

TWO MIRACULOUS FEEDINGS

Have you ever gone a few hours without eating any food? Sure you have. Maybe between breakfast and lunch, or between lunch and dinner. Certainly, you don't eat while you sleep!

But have you ever gone all day without food? No food when you woke up. No food for snack time. No food for lunch. No food after school. No food for dinner. No food before bed. Not even a midnight snack!

How hungry do you think you would be if you went all day without food? You might just be hungry enough to shout, "Mom! Dad! Anybody! I'm starving! Feed me."

One day Jesus found himself surrounded by a very hungry crowd. Some of them had eaten nothing all day. Jesus' best friends—the disciples—wanted to send all the people away. But Jesus had a more loving idea. He wanted to feed all the people right then and there. But how? How many fish and how many loaves of bread do you think you would need to feed 5,000 hungry men?

What if you wanted to feed 5,000 hungry families—moms, dads, and children? I would imagine it would take 20,000 fish and lots and lots of loaves. What if you only had two fish and five loaves? Could you feed the hungry crowd? No way! But that was all Jesus had. Two fish. Five loaves.

Now listen to what Jesus did next. Jesus told the crowd to sit down in the grass. What was He going to do? He took the five loaves and the two fish. With the food in his hands, He looked up to heaven and prayed.

Then something amazing happened. He handed the food to the disciples. They gave it to the people. And that was that. No! That wasn't that. The food kept coming from His hands! Two fish turned into ten fish. Ten turned into a hundred. A hundred turned into a thousand. A thousand into . . . well, you get the picture.

veryone ate. Everyone was full. They were so full that there were twelve baskets of bread left! This was a once in a lifetime miracle! Unless, of course, you're

Jesus.

MATTHEW 15: 13 - 21

When he went ashore he saw a great crowd, and he had compassion on them and healed their sick. Now when it was evening, the disciples came to him and said, "This is a desolate place, and the day is now over; send the crowds away to go into the villages and buy food for themselves." But Jesus said, "They need not go away; you give them something to eat." They said to him, "We have only five loaves here and two fish." And he said, "Bring them here to me." Then he ordered the crowds to sit down on the grass, and taking the five loaves and the two fish, he looked up to heaven and said a blessing. Then he broke the loaves and gave them to the disciples, and the disciples gave them to the crowds. And they all ate and were satisfied. And they took up twelve baskets full of the broken pieces left over. And those who ate were about five thousand men, besides women and children.

There was another time Jesus fed a large crowd. The second time the crowd was a bit smaller, but the miracle was just as big. With seven loaves and a few small fish Jesus fed "four thousand men, besides women and children" (Matthew 15:38). And this time there were leftovers too. Seven baskets filled with bread. Doggie bags for everyone!

MATTHEW 15: 32 - 39

Then Jesus called his disciples to him and said, "I have compassion on the crowd because they have been with me now three days and have nothing to eat. And I am unwilling to send them away hungry, lest they faint on the way." And the disciples said to him, "Where are we to get enough bread in such a desolate place to feed so great a crowd?" And Jesus said to them, "How many loaves do you have?" They said, "Seven, and a few small fish." And directing the crowd to sit down on the ground, he took the seven loaves and the fish, and having given thanks he broke them and gave them to the disciples, and the disciples gave them to the crowds. And they all ate and were satisfied. And they took up seven baskets full of the broken pieces left over. Those who ate were four thousand men, besides women and children.

CRUMBS FOR THE DOG

Now, between those two incredible meals, we read in God's Word about a hungry woman. Unlike the others, she wasn't hungry for food. She was hungry for a Savior. She needed Jesus to save her daughter from an awful sickness. Her daughter had evil spirits living inside her, what the Bible calls "demon possession." Scary, scary stuff.

This story begins with Jesus on a journey. He traveled from a place called Gennesaret to towns called Tyre and Sidon. Can you find these places on the map? The distance from Gennesaret to Tyre was thirty-five miles and from Tyre to Sidon was twenty-five more miles. How many miles is that?

Sixty!

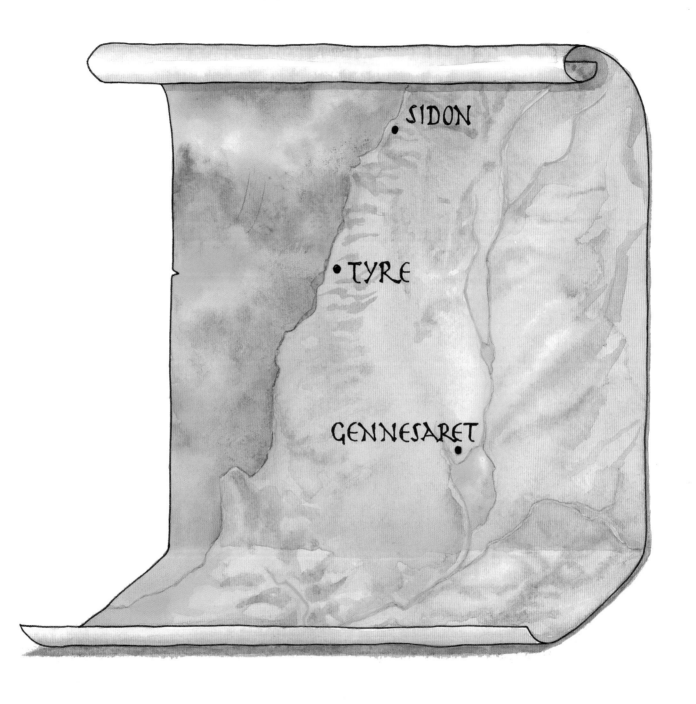

Now, how do you think Jesus got there? Did He drive? No, cars weren't invented then. Did He take the train or jump on a jet plane? No, of course not. Did He use some supersonic-speed skateboard? Now, let's not be silly. He walked, right? Yes, He walked and walked and walked. Then, He walked and walked and walked.

How long would it take you to walk sixty miles? It would take me three or four days, and I have really long legs.

Why was Jesus walking to Tyre and Sidon? Why not go to the big city of Rome, the beautiful city of Jericho, or the holy city of Jerusalem? And, besides, weren't the towns of Tyre and Sidon outside of the Promised Land? (They were.) And weren't these places where the people called Gentiles lived? (They were.) Then, wasn't this a very surprising place for Jesus—the Jewish Messiah—to go to? (It was!)

What is also very surprising is who Jesus met there. It wasn't a Roman king. It wasn't a Jewish priest. It wasn't even another hungry crowd. Look at what the Bible says:

"And behold, a Canaanite woman from that region came out. . ." (Matthew 15:21).

A woman! A Canaanite! Like the Egyptians and the Babylonians, the Canaanites were Israel's enemy. Yikes, who is this woman? And what does she want?

Well, she didn't want to harm Jesus, that's for sure. Instead, she wanted help. Remember—she had a very hungry heart because she had a very sick daughter.

So when she came to Jesus, she cried out, "Have mercy on me, O Lord, Son of David; my daughter is severely oppressed by a demon" (Matthew 15:21).

Now, what did Jesus do? Let's read what the Bible says next.

But Jesus did not answer her a word. And his disciples came and begged him, saying, "Send her away, for she is crying out after us." He answered, "I was sent only to the lost sheep of the house of Israel" (Matthew 15:23-24).

Wow! What strange responses. The disciples seemed annoyed with her. "Why is she making so much noise? She is bothering us. Jesus, send her home!" Even Jesus seemed not to care for her. At first He said nothing.

Then, when He did talk, He said something quite odd. He talked about being sent to "the lost sheep of the house of Israel." What did He mean by that? Well, He meant that He was the Jewish Savior and that He was sent to help the Jews, who, like lost sheep needed to find their way home.

So, hearing what the disciples and Jesus said, what do you think might happen next? Would she walk away? No way! Did she look for someone else to feed her hungry heart and heal her daughter? Not at all.

Instead, she moved closer to Jesus. She knelt before him. She cried out again, "Lord, help me." Her daughter was filled with evil spirits. She needed Jesus' good power to destroy Satan's evil power.

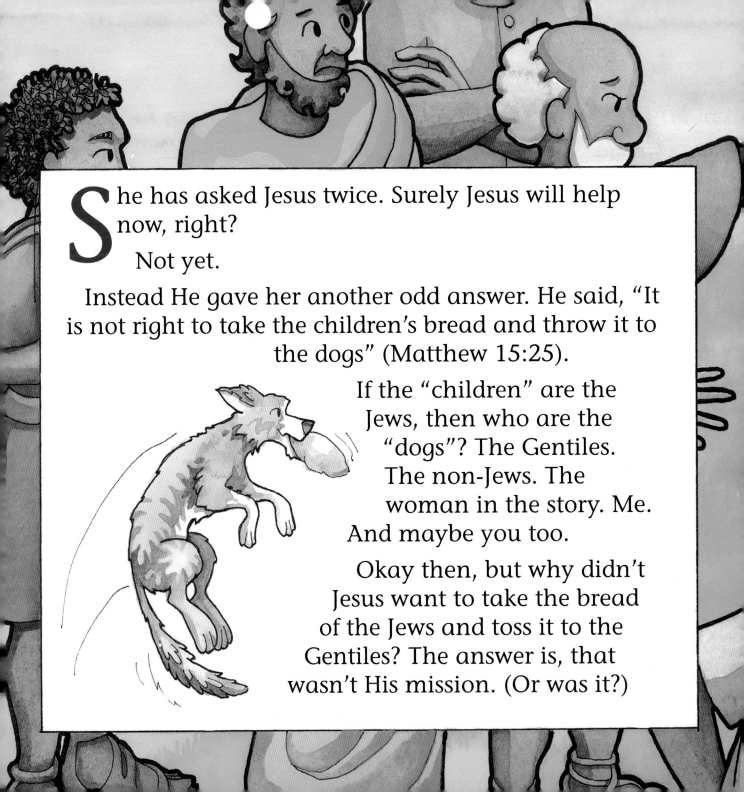

She has asked Jesus twice. Surely Jesus will help now, right?

Not yet.

Instead He gave her another odd answer. He said, "It is not right to take the children's bread and throw it to the dogs" (Matthew 15:25).

If the "children" are the Jews, then who are the "dogs"? The Gentiles. The non-Jews. The woman in the story. Me. And maybe you too.

Okay then, but why didn't Jesus want to take the bread of the Jews and toss it to the Gentiles? The answer is, that wasn't His mission. (Or was it?)

The story isn't over. Jesus hadn't finished. She hadn't finished either! She refused to give up hope. She knew her daughter was sick. She believed that Jesus was the "Lord." She trusted that He alone could and would help. So, she didn't give up.

"Yes, Lord," she said, "yet even the dogs eat the crumbs that fall from their masters' table" (v. 27).

She didn't deny that she was a "dog." She didn't insist that she deserved to be blessed. She acknowledged that she was helpless. She knew that crumbs from the master's meal was all that she needed. What a response!

Oh, but He wouldn't feed her crumbs that would leave her hungry. He would fill her completely up, just like the crowds who ate the fish and bread.

"Daughter, fill yourself up! It's all yours! Great is your faith! Be it done for you as you desire." And guess what? He didn't give her physical food. No, something better. "Her daughter was healed instantly" (v. 28). Without a touch, without a word, the girl was cured, rescued from the evil powers. Isn't that amazing? And so awesome!

So what was The Dog's Dinner? It wasn't food. It was Jesus Himself! It was His peace, His love, and His righteousness.

And this "dog" was fed–and fed well. Why? Because she believed in Jesus. Her faith was great. It was great because she wouldn't give up. It was great because she called Jesus, "Lord, Son of David." She believed that Jesus was the king, the ruler of all creation and over all people.

It was great because she asked for mercy. She knew that only Jesus could conquer the devil and heal her daughter. It was great because she came to Jesus alone, with faith alone. Do you have such faith? If not, ask God to give it to you. He loves to give that gift! He loves to give his gift of faith as much as he loves to give his people good food.

When Jesus walked on earth He gave His people a sign that He was the promised Savior and that He loved them. He fed them food! He fed the Jews. He fed the Gentiles. He fed men, women, and children. He fed everyone who came to Him for life!

And one day, when we see Him face to face, He will feed us the greatest meal in history. There will be bread and fish. There will be milk and honey. There will be every kind of fruit from the fruit trees. Oh, what a happy day that will be. We will be so full. Full of God's love for us. Full of His good food!

MATTHEW 15: 21-28

THE FAITH OF A CANAANITE WOMAN

And Jesus went away from there and withdrew to the district of Tyre and Sidon. And behold, a Canaanite woman from that region came out and was crying, "Have mercy on me, O Lord, Son of David; my daughter is severely oppressed by a demon." But he did not answer her a word. And his disciples came and begged him, saying, "Send her away, for she is crying out after us." He answered, "I was sent only to the lost sheep of the house of Israel." But she came and knelt before him, saying, "Lord, help me." And he answered, "It is not right to take the children's bread and throw it to the dogs." She said, "Yes, Lord, yet even the dogs eat the crumbs that fall from their masters' table." Then Jesus answered her, "O woman, great is your faith! Be it done for you as you desire." And her daughter was healed instantly.

What is the world's biggest question?

"Is the moon really made of cheese?" No. "Why can't I hit my sister if she hit me first?" No. "Why do I have to brush my baby teeth if they're just going to fall out?" No. No. No.

"What must I do to inherit eternal life?" Yes, that is the world's biggest question. "How do I get to heaven? How do I live with God forever and ever and ever?"

Find out how Jesus answered this question with a camel, a needle. and two rich men!

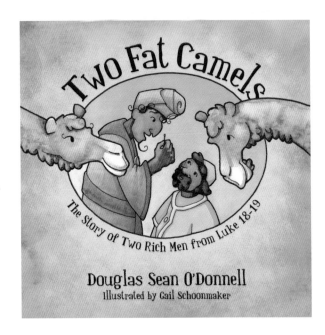

Two Fat Camels

The Story of Two Rich Men from Luke 18-19

Douglas Sean O'Donnell
Illustrated by Gail Schoonmaker

Two Fat Camels belongs on the reading shelf
of young children!
David Helm, Author of *The Big Picture Story Bible*

... a book that will delight and instruct children ...
Warmly recommended!
Justin Taylor, author and blogger,
Between Two Worlds, Wheaton, Illinois

ISBN: 978-1-78191-562-2

DEDICATION

To my father, Patrick. DSO
To Sammy and David, with love. GKS

Christian Focus Publications publishes books for adults and children under its four main imprints: Christian Focus, CF4K, Mentor and Christian Heritage. Our books reflect our conviction that God's Word is reliable and Jesus is the way to know him, and live for ever with him.

Our children's publication list includes a Sunday School curriculum that covers pre-school to early teens, and puzzle and activity books. We also publish personal and family devotional titles, biographies and inspirational stories that children will love. If you are looking for quality Bible teaching for children, then we have an excellent range of Bible stories and age-specific theological books. From pre-school board books to teenage apologetics, we have it covered!

Find us at our web page: www.christianfocus.com

10 9 8 7 6 5 4 3 2 1

Copyright © 2016 Douglas Sean O'Donnell

ISBN: 978-1-78191-746-6

Published by Christian Focus Publications, Geanies House, Fearn, Tain, Ross-shire, IV20 1TW, Scotland, U.K.

Cover design: Daniel van Straaten. Illustrations: Gail Schoonmaker

Printed in China